Where Can You Shop?

Cory Phillips

You can shop in different kinds of stores.

grocery store

hardware store

bakery

shoe store

toy store

Where can you shop for **food**?

You can shop for food at a **grocery store**.

Where can you shop for **shoes**?

You can shop for shoes at a **shoe store**.

Where can you shop for **bread**?

You can shop for bread at a **bakery**.

Where can you
shop for **tools**?

You can shop for tools at a **hardware store.**

Where can you shop for **toys**?

You can shop for toys at a **toy store**.